Nature's Patchwork Quilt

Understanding Habitats

Mary Miché

Illustrations by
Consie Powell

DAWN PUBLICATIONS

DEDICATIONS

To all teachers, especially Evelyn Miché, reading specialist,
and Margaret Miché, second grade. — MM

For Steve and Sally and Brian - the other three squares to my four-patch. — CP

SPECIAL THANKS TO

Esther Railton Rice, Marion Kaiser, Debra Bragg, Roger A. Powell,
Barbara Mims, David Silver, Nate and Andrew Secrest.
In Memory of Steve Medley, Yosemite Association

Library of Congress Cataloging-in-Publication Data

Miché, Mary.
 Nature's patchwork quilt : understanding habitats / by Mary Miché ;
illustrated by Consie Powell. -- 1st ed.
  p. cm.
 Includes bibliographical references.
  ISBN 978-1-58469-169-3 (hbk.) -- ISBN 978-1-58469-170-9 (pbk.) 1.
Habitat (Ecology)--Juvenile literature. 2. Natural history--Juvenile
literature. 3. Nature--Juvenile literature. 4. Nature study--Activity
programs--Juvenile literature I. Powell, Consie, ill. II. Title.
 QH541.14.M53 2012
 577--dc23

                    2011048064

Book design and production by Patty Arnold, *Menagerie Design & Publishing*

Manufactured by Regent Publishing Services, Hong Kong
Printed May, 2012, in ShenZhen, Guangdong, China
10 9 8 7 6 5 4 3 2 1
First Edition

DAWN PUBLICATIONS

12402 Bitney Springs Road
Nevada City, CA 95959
530-274-7775
nature@dawnpub.com

Look into nature and you will see
a patchwork of beauty and mystery.

A patchwork quilt
has many pieces that
fit together to make
a beautiful blanket.

Nature is like a patchwork quilt.
It has many different habitats
all pieced together to create
our wonderful planet.

In a habitat, such as a forest,
animals and plants live together.
They are food for each other
and help the forest grow
and develop.

Each plant or animal
depends on others, like a
quilt stitched together.
We call this **interdependence**.

A desert is another habitat,
with plants and animals that can
live in a hot and dry climate.

In a quilt, each piece has its own unique place in the design. In a habitat, each animal and plant has a special role, called its **niche**.

A **prairie** is a grassland habitat. Some prairies have prairie dogs that eat roots and plants. Snakes eat the prairie dogs. Hawks eat the snakes.

This is called a **food chain**. The prairie plants are the first link, prairie dogs are second, snakes are third, and hawks, at the top of the food chain, are the fourth link.

The ocean, which has 97% of all the water on Earth, has many different habitats. Ocean water near the surface contains very tiny plants called **phytoplankton**.

Tiny animals called **zooplankton** eat phytoplankton. Tiny shrimp called krill eat zooplankton. Little fish called sardines eat krill. Salmon eat sardines. Sharks or seals eat salmon. This is one **marine food chain**.

The seashore at the edge of the ocean also has many habitats. Different plants and animals live in the shallow water, on the rocks, and in the sand.

Over generations, plants and animals often change in ways that help them survive. For instance, the feet of swimming birds changed to have webbing, which help them swim better than their ancestors did. Some fish can change colors to help them hide, or **camouflage**, themselves. Such changes are called **adaptations**.

Lakes and ponds have many tiny plants and animals living in them. They are very small, but you can see them with a magnifying glass or a special tool called a **microscope**.

These microscopic plants and
animals are food for each other.
The way that these plants and animals
eat and are eaten is so complicated
that we call it a **food web**.

Arctic and high mountain habitats are very cold much of the year. It's a tough place to live. To survive harsh climates, plants either stay alive all winter under snow or make seeds that can survive the cold.

Animals store up food to survive in burrows or hibernate in caves. Birds fly to warmer places. Ways of adjusting to the climate are called **survival mechanisms**.

Rainforest habitats are very wet. Cool rainforests are **temperate**, such as in North America and New Zealand. Hot rainforests are **tropical**, such as in South America, Africa, and southern Asia.

Many rainforest trees are large. Many are cut down. This is called **deforestation**. Fewer places are left for plants and animals that can only survive in a rainforest.

Rainforests have lots and lots and
LOTS of different kinds of trees, shrubs,
mosses, lichens, fungi, insects, reptiles,
amphibians, birds and mammals.
Many different species together
make up **biodiversity**.

Houses, towns, and cities are habitats for people. People built them over what once was a prairie, desert, forest, or rainforest. People have changed some plants and animals by working with them over generations.

Dogs, cats, and farm animals, as well as many plants that produce food, are very different from their wild ancestors. When plants and animals are changed by people we call it **domestication**.

Ranches and farms are also habitats made by people on what was once prairie, forest, or desert. Often domesticated animals like cows, horses, pigs, and chickens live there. Domesticated plants like tomatoes, corn, and wheat also grow there.

More and more natural habitats are being taken over by human habitats. When a natural habitat is gone

and plants or animals don't have any place left to live, they die. When the last plant or animal of a species dies, the species is **extinct**.

Margaret Wentworth Owings

Jane Goodall

David Suzuki

Archie Carr

Rachel Carson

Because plants and animals can't speak for themselves, many **environmentalists** have worked hard to save them by preserving their habitats.

Margaret Murie

Roger Tory Peterson

Eugenie Clark

John Muir

Sylvia Earle

Ronald "RD" Lawrence

Jay Norwood "Ding" Darling

Aldo Leopold

Theodore Roosevelt

Henry David Thoreau

Roger Payne

They clean up rivers,
plant trees,
help animals,
study science,
paint pictures,
sing songs,
write books,

give speeches,
make movies,
persuade policy-makers,
give money,
organize friends,
and much more.

Edward O. Wilson

Wangari Maathai

Jacques-Yves Cousteau

William Temple Hornaday

Tierney Thys

When you are in nature,
look around at its beauty.
Consider how all the plants
and animals live together in an
interdependent web of life.

This patchwork quilt of
nature covers the whole
Earth, your home. It is yours
to learn about, to enjoy,
to care for, and to love.

Tips from the Author

How will you care for our Earth?

Encourage children to talk about what they love about the earth and ask them to draw pictures of themselves doing an activity that shows how much they care, such as planting flowers, feeding birds, or picking up litter. Students may write a sentence describing what they are doing in the pictures. Preschoolers may dictate a sentence.

Become an Animal Expert

Ask children to become an expert about an animal that lives nearby. Bring in books and magazines for children to use to get information. Children can share what they learn with the whole class.

Fun Activities

The following are some of the activities you can find at **www.dawnpub. com**. Click on "Teachers/Librarians" and "Downloadable Activities."

🍃 There are lots of animals and plants on every page and you can have fun finding them all. On the first page (page 3, clockwise from upper right) are a dragonfly, grizzly bears, aster leaf, ducklings, lichen, blue jay, moth, Pacific herring, toad, kelp, loon, snake, skunk, spider, turtle, squirrel, cicada, quail, shrew, mushroom, and anemone. In the "I Spy Animals" activity you can find a list of animals and their precise names for each page in this book.

🍃 This book introduces important vocabulary, from adaptation to zooplankton. In "Wonderful Wild Words" is a list of key words and ideas on how to teach them.

🍃 Choose one of the black and white pages on the website to build a diorama of a habitat. Color the page and use it as the backdrop for a diorama. You can make the animals out of clay. You can also use the black and white pages for other coloring activities or for making a jig-saw puzzle. See "Creating Nature Play."

🔍 There are lots of kids hidden in the patchwork quilts. How many can you find? "Where's the Wilderness Kid?" on the website will tell you the answer.

Nature Math Concepts

As you read the book for a second or third time, you can point out the symmetry of the art and discuss that concept. You can also download a black and white page from the website, color it, and create a categorization activity. For example, using the forest habitat (pages 6-7), your students can color mammals red, birds blue, reptiles yellow, insects brown and amphibians green. You can also create a bar graph showing how many kinds of animals are on the page. Repeat this activity with other pages.

Learn about great environmentalists

The environmentalists pictured on pages 26 and 27 are all chosen from *Earth Heroes*, a book series from Dawn Publications which contains short, highly interesting biographies of many of the world's leading naturalists, including stories of their youth. After reading the biographies, select stories that will appeal to your students. You can make the stories really come alive with a simple prop. Simple props might include a walking stick for John Muir, a seashell for Rachel Carson, a duck call for Ding Darling, or a field guide for Roger Tory Peterson.

> 🌿 *Earth Heroes: Champions of the Wilderness* portrays David Suzuki, Aldo Leopold, Theodore Roosevelt, Henry David Thoreau, Margaret Murie, Wangari Maathai, and John Muir.

> 🐚 *Earth Heroes: Champions of the Ocean* portrays Margaret Wentworth Owings, Archie Carr, Roger Payne, Eugenie Clark, Sylvia Earle, Jacques-Yves Cousteau, and Tierney Thys.

> 🍃 *Earth Heroes: Champions of Wild Animals* portrays Jane Goodall, Jay Norwood "Ding" Darling, Rachel Carson, Roger Tory Peterson, Edward O. Wilson, Ronald "RD" Lawrence, and William Temple Hornaday.

Where are the rainforests?

Did you know there are rainforests all over the world? Find pictures and information about tropical rainforests at **www.marietta.edu/~biol/biomes/troprain.htm**. To learn about temperate rainforests, go to **www.marietta.edu/~biol/biomes/temprain.htm**.

Animal Food Chain Play

Designate the boundaries of a large playing area outside. Choose one of the habitats from the book and four elements in a food chain. Assign students to play the roles of one of the parts of the chain. For example, the prairie habitat includes prairie plants (about half of the students), prairie dogs (slightly less than half of the remaining students), snakes (several students) and hawks (two or three students). Plants are given two bandanas, which they hold in their hands. Prairie dogs and snakes are given one bandana to tuck into a back pocket. Hawks, at the top of the food chain, don't receive a bandana. The object of the game is for the prairie dogs to eat as many plants as they can before being eaten by a snake. The snakes try to eat as many prairie dogs as they can without being eaten by a hawk. To play, have plants spread out throughout the playing area, lie down on their backs, and wave their bandanas. At the sound of your signal, the food chain is set into motion as prairie dogs, snakes, and hawks run onto the field to grab bandanas. Signal the end of the round once all of the plants have been eaten. Switch roles and play another round. After playing, discuss the importance of each part of the food chain.

Musical Accompaniments:

Mary Miché has two environmental education recordings: "Nature Nuts" and "Earthy Tunes." These can be found at **www.marymiche.com**. The songs from "Nature Nuts" that particularly complement this book are "Nature's Niches," "Romp in the Swamp," "All God's Critters," and "Newts, Salamanders and Frogs." The songs from "Earthy Tunes" that reinforce the ideas of nature appreciation are "Spiders and Snakes," "Banana Slug," "Turtle," "Six Plant Parts," and "Bugs in Your Bark."

Mary Miché has been an environmental educator since 1972, when she began her work in outdoor education schools. She completed her masters degree in environmental education in 1982. She has visited hundreds of schools since then, singing her nature and science songs for children. This book was inspired by her many trips to and concerts in Yosemite National Park. Mary has worked with children in public schools for over thirty years. She is especially concerned with helping children to understand environmental processes and to take care of our earth. **www.MaryMiche.com**

Consie Powell loves to "muck around in nature's lovely untidy places," as she puts it, and then to illustrate the complexities of nature. She has spent time in all of the habitats illustrated in this book, her trusty sketchbook and a small tin of watercolors in hand. She has illustrated a dozen children's picture books about nature, seven of which she also wrote. Although she grew up in sunny southern California, Consie now lives in the far north woods of Minnesota with her husband and their Newfoundland dogs. **www.ConsiePowell.com**

Some Other Nature Appreciation Books You Might Like

Over in the Ocean: In a Coral Reef is a delightful, energetic counting and singing introduction to ocean animals, part of a best-selling series that also includes *Over in the Jungle, Over in the Arctic, Over in the Forest*, and *Over in Australia*. **THIS BOOK IS NOW AVAILABLE AS AN APP!**

In the Trees, Honey Bees offers a inside-the-hive view of a wild colony, along with solid information about these remarkable and valuable creatures.

Molly's Organic Farm is based on the true story of homeless cat that found herself in the wondrous world of an organic farm. Seen through Molly's eyes, the reader discovers the interplay of nature that grows wholesome food.

Jo MacDonald Had a Garden and *Jo MacDonald Saw a Pond* are delightful gardener's (and nature-lover's) variations on "Old MacDonald Had a Farm." Jo is Old MacDonald's granddaughter and his farm is such a cool place. E—I—E—I—O!

A Drop Around the World and *Pass the Energy, Please!* both are favorites with teachers, presenting the water cycle and the food cycle in wonderfully visual, understandable fashion.

Eliza and the Dragonfly is a charming story revolving around the beauty and wonder of the hidden world that can be found in a local pond.

Dawn Publications is dedicated to inspiring in children a deeper understanding and appreciation for all life on Earth. You can browse through our titles, download resources for teachers, and order at **www.dawnpub.com** or call 800-545-7475.